SNOW LEOPARDS

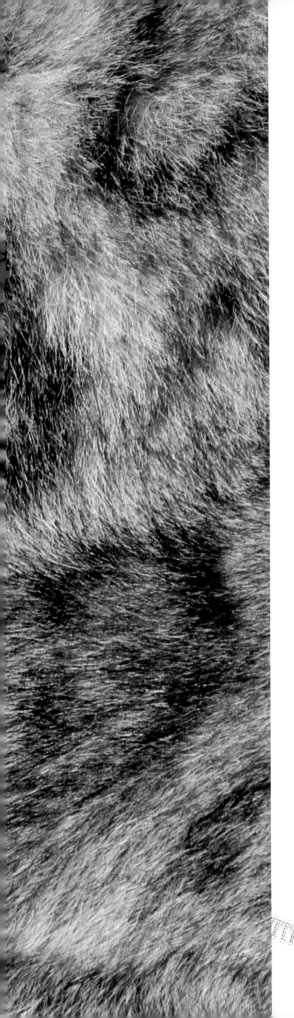

LIVING WILD

Published by Creative Education and Creative Paperbacks
P.O. Box 227, Mankato, Minnesota 56002
Creative Education and Creative Paperbacks are imprints of The Creative Company.
www.thecreativecompany.us

Design and production by Mary Herrmann
Art direction by Rita Marshall
Printed in China

Photographs by Alamy (AF archive/Alamy Stock Photo), Corbis (Jane Sweeney/JAI), Creative Commons Wikimedia (Derzsi Elekes Andor, Dragoman, Ksuryawanshi, A. Moscovets, Trisha Shears, Vassil), Dreamstime (Joaquín Álvarez, Lukas Blazek, Anshuman Datta, Mikael Males, Misad), iStockphoto (abzerit, belizar73, gui00878, oorka), Shutterstock (andamanec, belizar, cpaulfell, Dennis W. Donohue, Helen E. Grose, Victoria Hillman, Jeannette Katzir Photog, Alan Jeffery, Vasiliy Koval, Elena Mirage, My Good Images, Byelikova Oksana, Bernhard Richter, SIHASAKPRACHUM, Peter Wey, Vladimir Wrangel, xtrekx, Abeselom Zerit)

Library of Congress Cataloging-in-Publication Data
Gish, Melissa.
Snow leopards / Melissa Gish.
p. cm. — (Living wild)
Includes bibliographical references and index.
Summary: A look at snow leopards, including their habitats, physical characteristics such as their retractable claws, behaviors, relationships with humans, and their ability to survive changing climates in the world today.

ISBN 978-1-60818-710-2 (hardcover)
ISBN 978-1-62832-306-1 (pbk)
ISBN 978-1-56660-746-9 (eBook)
1. Snow leopard—Juvenile literature. I. Title. II. Series: Living wild.

QL737.C23G5175 2016
599.75'55—dc23   2015026826

CCSS: RI.5.1, 2, 3, 8; RST.6-8.1, 2, 5, 6, 8; RH.6-8.3, 4, 5, 6, 7, 8

First Edition HC 9 8 7 6 5 4 3 2 1
First Edition PBK 9 8 7 6 5 4 3 2 1

CREATIVE EDUCATION • CREATIVE PAPERBACKS

SNOW LEOPARDS

Melissa Gish

Just after dawn in northern India's Hemis National Park, a snow leopard steps silently down the

mountainside. The ghostly cat's coat hides it
from the bharal that dot the rocky ledges.

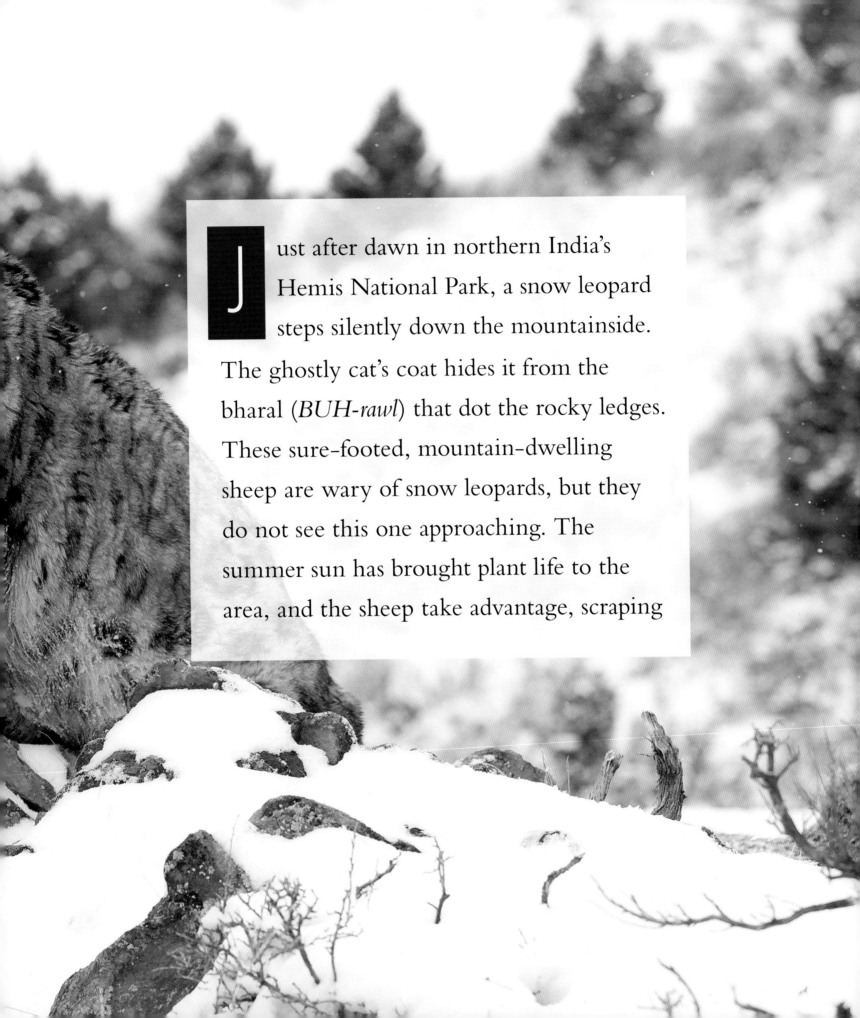

J ust after dawn in northern India's Hemis National Park, a snow leopard steps silently down the mountainside. The ghostly cat's coat hides it from the bharal (*BUH-rawl*) that dot the rocky ledges. These sure-footed, mountain-dwelling sheep are wary of snow leopards, but they do not see this one approaching. The summer sun has brought plant life to the area, and the sheep take advantage, scraping

moss from the surface of the rocks. They nibble the stitchwort and saxifrage that struggle to grow around jagged boulders. The snow leopard tracks one of the smaller bharal, slipping behind a boulder each time the sheep glances up from its meal. Suddenly, the snow leopard pounces on the bharal's back, crushing the animal's spine. The snow leopard will drag its kill back up the mountain to bury it in the snow—a meal that will last several days.

WHERE IN THE WORLD THEY LIVE

■ **Snow Leopard**
central Asia, mainly
the Hindu Kush
and Himalayas

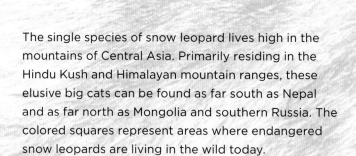

The single species of snow leopard lives high in the
mountains of Central Asia. Primarily residing in the
Hindu Kush and Himalayan mountain ranges, these
elusive big cats can be found as far south as Nepal
and as far north as Mongolia and southern Russia. The
colored squares represent areas where endangered
snow leopards are living in the wild today.

BUILT FOR THE COLD

Snow leopards have keen eyesight that is six times stronger than human eyesight.

As big cats and members of the Felidae family, snow leopards, jaguars, leopards, lions, and tigers also belong to the genus *Panthera*. In Greek, the word *pan* means "all," and *thera* means "beast," so the name describes beasts that hunt all other animals. Snow leopards live in 12 countries throughout Central Asia. Most snow leopards are found in the Hindu Kush and the Himalayas—high, rugged mountains of south-central Asia. There the cats **migrate** between altitudes of 6,500 feet (1,981 m) in winter and 17,000 feet (5,182 m) in summer. Others remain at lower elevations, around 3,281 feet (1,000 m), year round in Russia and Mongolia.

Snow leopards prefer steep mountainsides covered with cliffs, ridges, caves, and rocky outcroppings where they can hide. Because snow leopards are found in such harsh habitats, they are difficult to study. Only a handful of researchers has conducted in-depth studies of snow leopards, and only recently has information about their hunting and mating behaviors come to light. Scientists estimate their numbers to be between 3,500 and 5,000. They are thinly distributed in **fragmented** habitats

Snow leopards regularly prey on bharal, also called blue sheep, which weigh 77 to 165 pounds (34.9–74.8 kg).

The snow leopard's uniquely long, heavy tail serves a number of valuable purposes.

The snow leopard's coat pattern is so complex and its fur so long that its spots appear to change as it walks.

covering an area of approximately 2 million square miles (5,179,976 sq km), roughly the size of Mexico. About 60 percent of snow leopards live in China.

The world's snow leopard population continues to decline mainly because of **poaching**, effects of global **climate change**, and shrinking prey populations. About 600 snow leopards are protected in zoos throughout the world. Many institutions actively sponsor **captive-breeding** programs. Since 1976, records of captive snow leopards have been kept in an international studbook, which is a way of tracking the family relationships of all the captive snow leopards in the world. Such records help institutions share snow leopards for breeding.

Snow leopards weigh 77 to 121 pounds (34.9–54.9 kg), with males up to 30 percent heavier than females. Both males and females stand about 24 inches (61 cm) tall at the shoulder and can grow to be 3 to 4.8 feet (0.9–1.5 m) from head to rump. The tail, which can be up to 40 inches (102 cm) long, provides balance as the snow leopard maneuvers sharply while running up and down the mountainside. Except for size, males and females look the same. The snow leopard's coloration

Though they are solitary animals in the wild, snow leopards in zoos show close pair bonding.

Like most of their feline relatives, snow leopards are constantly on the lookout for prey during waking hours.

helps it blend in with its surroundings. Its fur is cream, yellowish, and smoky gray, speckled with dark-gray to black spots and dark, ringed markings called rosettes. No two snow leopards have the same markings. Like human fingerprints, each snow leopard's rosettes are unique. Though their coat does little to hide them against snow, the spotted pattern helps snow leopards blend into rocky surroundings as they sneak up on prey.

In an effort to rebuild the Himalayan wolf's population, some individuals are protected in Indian zoos.

Snow leopards have no natural enemies besides humans. At the top of their **food chain**, these cats share their habitats and food sources with only one other major predator: the wolf. About 350 critically endangered Himalayan wolves compete with snow leopards in northern India. Abundant Tibetan wolves (a subspecies of gray wolf) share much of the snow leopards' habitat from Kazakhstan to China. Since snow leopards are more powerful hunters, wolves often wait for the big cats to hide their meals, and then they steal the food.

Powerful chest muscles help snow leopards climb steep mountains and run after swift prey such as hares, wild boars, and Himalayan tahrs (fleet-footed mountain goats). They can take down prey three times their own weight,

Many scientists search for decades without ever seeing the highly elusive snow leopard.

During the fall mating season for mountain goats and sheep, the distracted animals fall prey to snow leopards.

usually by leaping from above. The snow leopard's powerful jaws pierce the victim's throat, cutting off its air supply, while long, **retractable** claws hold the animal still until it suffocates. Snow leopards are most successful while hunting on rocky mountainsides, where their stealth and camouflage are advantageous. They are more challenged on snow- and ice-covered mountainsides, where they cannot see their footing and may slip.

Sparsely inhabited, with little vegetation or running water, snow leopard habitat is virtually silent except for the sound of the wind. The cliffs are so steep that one misstep could dislodge a rock and alert prey to the snow leopard's presence. Snow leopards must be silent stalkers and swift to ambush. Short front limbs and long, powerful back limbs help snow leopards leap 30 feet (9.1 m)—more than 6 times their body length—in a single stride. Their broad, rounded paws have large pads surrounded by thick fur. The paws act like snowshoes to help the big cats grip slippery rock surfaces and quietly walk over snow without sinking.

The snow leopard has many qualities that help it survive in the cold. To minimize heat loss, its ears are short, and its thick tail can be wrapped around its face like a scarf.

Without its long, rudder-like tail, the snow leopard would not be able to accurately leap great distances.

Researchers at New York's Hunter College found that snow leopards are naturally curious and playful.

The hair covering the snow leopard's belly grows as long as five inches (12.7 cm) and thickens during the fall and winter months. At an elevation of 9,800 feet (2,987 m), the air contains only two-thirds as much oxygen as it does at sea level. At 17,000 feet (5,182 m), there is roughly half the oxygen content in the air. The snow leopard's wide nostrils can take in lots of air. In addition, the snow leopard has a short muzzle (the area that includes the nose and mouth). This allows the nasal (nose) cavity to heat frigid air before it reaches the cat's powerful lungs.

Snow leopards are crepuscular animals, which means they are most active during the twilight hours of dawn and dusk. Like other big cats, snow leopards have eyes with round pupils that provide excellent vision, particularly in low light. But unlike their relatives, snow leopards' eyes are pale green or gray. They are equipped with a reflective layer of tissue called a tapetum lucidum. This tissue collects light and concentrates it in the center of the **retina**, allowing the snow leopard to see twice as well in low light as it can in daylight. The tissue also causes eyeshine, making the eyes reflect color when a light is shined on them. The snow leopard's eyeshine is greenish-white.

The snow leopard has been named the official national animal of Afghanistan, Kazakhstan, and Pakistan.

Cats, including snow leopards, often yawn out of contentment and not because they are tired or bored.

MOUNTAIN CATS

Like most cats, snow leopards sleep on and off for 12 to 20 hours during each 24-hour period. They sleep in caves and rock crevices, protected from wind and snowfall. They also doze while perched on high cliffs or ridges, where they can scan the area below for prey. Snow leopards eat slowly, often taking up to four days to consume a meal. Prey that is too large to drag up a mountainside is left at the kill site, and the snow leopard will remain close to it, protecting it from scavenging wolves. Snow leopards help keep herds of goats and sheep healthy by targeting the weak, old, and ill. While large prey is preferred, snow leopards will eat anything they can catch, including mice, as a small snack.

Unlike lions and tigers, snow leopards do not roar. Snow leopards are mostly silent, other than hissing and growling during rare fights and wailing during mating season to indicate their willingness to mate. Snow leopards also communicate by chuffing. Produced when the mouth is closed and air is snorted through the nostrils, chuffing is similar to purring in **domesticated** cats but lower in tone. Mating pairs, mothers and offspring, and

No prey is too small for the snow leopard, which needs to eat frequently to help maintain its body temperature.

By preying on Himalayan marmots, snow leopards prevent the rodents from eating too much vegetation.

Where prey is readily available, snow leopards typically share territory without conflict.

adults crossing paths without a fight may exchange this sort of friendly greeting with one another.

The snow leopard is a solitary animal, living alone in a particular area called its home range. The size of a home range varies from 30 to 65 square miles (77.7–168 sq km) where prey is abundant to more than 1,000 square miles (2,590 sq km) where prey is scarce. Home ranges may overlap, and, unlike most other big cats, snow leopards simply avoid each other rather than defend the borders of their home ranges. To keep from running into one another, snow leopards mark their boundaries by dropping piles of waste matter, called scat, and by spraying urine and rubbing scent from **glands** in their faces on the undersides of rock outcroppings. They also scratch rock faces and dig up patches of earth to leave scent marks from glands in their feet.

Such messages contain information about which cats visited the area and when they were there. Snow leopards travel all around their territory, marking the boundaries every few days to give each other time to move on so that they can avoid contact. They rarely stay in one part of their home range for more than a few weeks. Only during mating season do snow leopards make an effort to contact each other. Females examine the rocks and leave special scents that indicate readiness to mate. Instead of "stay away" messages, these are "come find me" messages. Normally, snow leopards stay a three days' to a week's walk away from each other, but they move closer as mating season approaches.

Mating season runs from January to mid-March. Females will wail loudly to draw the attention of males. A male and female come together for several days, mating many times to ensure success. During their time together, they may hunt as a team—the only time of year when adult

Snow leopards usually remain hidden among rocks unless they are chasing down prey.

Snow leopard cubs are three months old when they first venture out of the den with their mother.

snow leopards share food. After mating, the male leaves the female, and they go about their solitary lives once more. As the babies (called cubs) develop inside her and the spring snowmelt begins, the female moves to a higher elevation and searches for a suitable den. In this cave or deep crevice, protected from the wind, she will give birth.

Offspring develop inside their mother for 93 to 110 days. In June or July, the female gives birth to two or three cubs that weigh one to one and a half pounds (0.5–0.7 kg). Like domesticated kittens, snow leopard cubs are born blind and toothless. As **mammals**, they immediately begin feeding on the milk produced by their mother. In about seven days, the cubs' eyes open, but they are still helpless. When they are about two months old, their mother begins feeding them solid food that she brings to the den. In another month, they follow their mother out of the den to explore the world.

At five months old, cubs no longer need their mother's milk, but they remain dependent on her until they are a year old. A yearling cub needs as much food as its mother, so great pressure is put on the mother to hunt almost daily if she has more than one cub. For 18 to 22 months, young snow leopards remain by their mother's side, learning

A bonded pair of snow leopards hunts, eats, and sleeps together for several days during mating season.

Snow leopard cubs are born with bright blue eyes that change to light green or gray as the cats age.

everything they will need to know for survival. This is the only point in a snow leopard's life when it will live and hunt with other snow leopards for an extended period of time.

When snow leopards are about two years old, their mother will chase them away. The young cats go off alone in search of unclaimed or abandoned territories. A female cub may be allowed to take a portion of her mother's home range and make it her own, but males must move farther away so as not to be in competition with older males in the area. They may travel as far as 100 miles (161 km) from their birthplace to establish their own home ranges. Females will be ready to mate by the time they are two to three years old, while males mature at about age four.

Because snow leopards are difficult to study, it is not known for sure how long they live in the wild. Teeth from snow leopards that had died of natural causes have been determined to be 10 to 15 years old. Snow leopards in captivity have lived as long as 22 years. Snow leopards face few natural perils, yet they have been classified as an endangered species by the International Union for Conservation of Nature (IUCN) since 1988 because of threats from human interference.

Twin births are common, but with triplets, protective parenting becomes a greater challenge.

Like domesticated cats, snow leopards may nibble plants and grass to help them cleanse their digestive systems.

Snow leopards are more active during daylight hours in areas where humans are not present.

GHOST OF THE MOUNTAINS

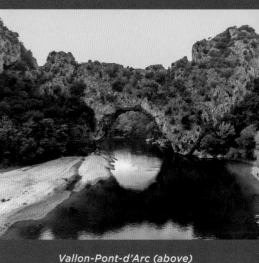

Vallon-Pont-d'Arc (above) is one area in France where visitors can see prehistoric art in caves.

Since earliest times, people have considered the elusive snow leopard to be a spiritual animal. It has been nicknamed the "Ghost of the Mountains." In some **cultures**, snow leopards were the pets of the mountain gods, and in others, the cats themselves were mysterious and powerful gods. Images of snow leopards appear in some of humankind's first artwork. In prehistoric times, the snow leopard's range was far greater. These cats existed with prehistoric humans throughout much of Europe, as evidenced by artwork of snow leopards created in present-day France.

Grotte Chauvet-Pont-d'Arc, discovered in 1994, is home to some of the world's oldest and best-preserved cave art. The walls of the cave are painted with more than 1,000 images of ice-age animals that include snow leopards, mammoths, bears, rhinos, bison, and aurochs (**extinct** ancestors of cattle). Many of the snow leopard images are close-ups of heads and necks featuring the snow leopard's distinctive short snout and small ears. The artwork, dating back 30,000 years, is considered a cultural treasure. It has been listed by the United Nations

Fourth- and 5th-century Scythian warriors wore ornaments featuring the snow leopard.

In 2011, a snow leopard was sighted in Russia's Sayano-Shushenskya Nature Reserve— the first in more than 30 years.

Educational, Scientific, and Cultural Organization (UNESCO) as a World Heritage Site, meaning it will be preserved and studied.

Early peoples also carved symbols and pictures into rocky cliffs and cave walls. Such carvings are called petroglyphs. In the 1990s, Dr. John Vincent Bellezza of the University of Virginia discovered petroglyphs in Changtang, one of the highest parts of the Tibetan Plateau. They had been created by the Zhang Zhung people between 900 and 600 B.C. Among the images carved onto rock walls was a scene depicting a snow leopard with gaping jaws chasing two wild sheep or goats under a crescent moon. Bellezza believes the scene may be not only an eyewitness account but also a symbolic depiction of the snow leopard's spiritual power.

The Scythians, a semi-**nomadic** people known for their exquisite golden ornaments and jewelry, inhabited much of Central Asia from the 7th century B.C. to the 4th century A.D. They specialized in images of animals, and one of the most famous discoveries of Scythian art was found in 1969 in southeastern Kazakhstan. The Issyk burial mound was the resting place of a king whose clothing was covered

with 4,000 golden ornaments shaped like birds, horses, mountain goats, and snow leopards.

By the 11th century, Buddhism had become the main religion in much of the snow leopard's Himalayan habitat. The first principle of Buddhism is reverence for all forms of life—even dangerous animals like snow leopards. These big cats became mystical symbols of the power of

A petroglyph from the 8th–5th century B.C. in Kyrgyzstan depicts hunters using tame snow leopards.

CHAPTER I. SIMLA

Below me the roofs of Simla glittered in the sunshine, and I stood on a level with the tops of the cedars; how delightful it was here far above the heavy sultry air of the plain. To the north, through a gap in the luxuriant woods, appeared a scene of incomparable beauty. There gleamed the nearest ranges of the Himalayas covered with eternal snow. The crest shone white against the turquoise-blue sky. The air was so clear that the distance seemed insignificant; only a few days' journey separated me from these mountains, and behind them lay mysterious Tibet, the forbidden land, the land of my dreams. Later on, towards mid-day, the air became hazy and the glorious view vanished, nor was it again visible during the few weeks I spent in Simla. It seemed as though a curtain had fallen between me and Tibet, and as though it had been vouchsafed to me to see only once from a distance the mountains over which the road led into the land of promise.

excerpt from Trans-Himalaya: Discoveries and Adventures in Tibet, *by Sven Hedin (1865–1952)*

nature. One Buddhist story tells of Milarepa, an 11th-century yogi (spiritual master) who was traveling around the villages of present-day Tibet's Qomolangma Nature Preserve when he got caught in a winter storm. He sought refuge in the Great Cave of Conquering Demons. While villagers searched for him, they observed a snow leopard watching them. The villagers could not find Milarepa all winter, and they assumed the snow leopard had killed him. In the spring, Milarepa returned to the village and explained that he was able to transform into the snow leopard to survive the winter.

The Wakhi people native to northern Pakistan, China, Tajikistan, and Afghanistan believe that powerful supernatural beings called *mergichan* inhabit the mountains and often take the form of snow leopards. The Dolpo people native to the borderlands of Nepal and Tibet tell stories of lamas, or Buddhist teachers, who travel to the mountains in the form of snow leopards to search for rare medicinal herbs. The Balti people of northern Pakistan and northern India view snow leopards as representing the land and all females, while otters are symbols of males and the water. According to Balti **mythology**, when

In 2007, the World Wildlife Fund sponsored a Russian stamp commemorating the snow leopard.

Snow leopards kill an average of one large animal twice a month, snacking on smaller prey between big meals.

Because *Kung Fu Panda*'s Tai Lung lacked humility, he could not be named the Dragon Warrior.

cubs are born, males join their fathers in the water, while females follow their mother into the mountains.

Some people in Nepal believe that snow leopards can remove the bad luck that people carry with them from past lives. Respecting and preserving snow leopards will allow these cats to work their magic. However, killing a snow leopard will transfer all the bad luck to the person who killed it. Respect for the snow leopard persists among most of the people who share its habitat. To this day, many farmers view snow leopards as protectors of the harvest. They believe that if snow leopards live in the area, the cats will keep other wild animals from invading fields and destroying crops.

Several nature and adventure books would not have been possible if not for the Nepalese and Tibetan people who assisted in the tracking of snow leopards. One of the first books to reveal some of the snow leopard's mysteries was *The Snow Leopard*, by naturalist Peter Matthiessen. He and biologist George Schaller traveled to Nepal in 1973. The 2012 book *Snow Leopard: Stories from the Roof of the World* is a collection of firsthand encounters with snow leopards in the Himalayas. And Eduard Fischer's 2014 book

Chasing the Phantom: In Pursuit of Myth and Meaning in the Realm of the Snow Leopard offers some of the latest biological information about these elusive cats as well as stories about their place in mythology.

Filming snow leopards in the wild is challenging. Their mountainous habitat is dangerous and unforgiving, and these cats are very difficult to find. Australian filmmaker Mitchell Kelly spent four years seeking snow leopards for the 2005 documentary "Silent Roar: Searching for the Snow Leopard," part of the BBC series *Nature*. Kelly was hospitalized twice and nearly lost his life in his quest to film snow leopards. Pakistani journalist Nisar Malik experienced a massive earthquake while filming snow leopards in the Hindu Kush, a mountain range that stretches between central Afghanistan and northern Pakistan. His film, *Snow Leopard: Beyond the Myth*, aired in 2008.

A much easier snow leopard to film was Tai Lung, a villainous character in the 2008 DreamWorks animated movie *Kung Fu Panda*. Tai Lung, which means "Great Dragon" in Chinese, has supernatural strength. However, he is defeated by Po, a pudgy panda who becomes a master of martial arts.

Snow leopards' teeth can grow to be one and a half inches (3.8 cm) in length by adulthood.

A snow leopard with rabies once attacked two men in 1940, but no healthy snow leopard has ever attacked a human.

Ama Dablam is a Himalayan mountain whose name means "mother's necklace" in Nepalese.

REVEALING SECRETS

The first true cats, or felids, **evolved** in Asia about 25 million years ago. They were small—about the size of a weasel. As they scattered around the world, they changed to suit the varying environments. Some grew larger, and by about 6 million years ago, the first big cats emerged. Scientists once thought big cats originated in Africa 3.6 million years ago. However, in 2010, a team of researchers led by Dr. Zhijie Jack Tseng, a **paleontologist** with the American Museum of Natural History in New York, made a discovery that pushed big cat evolution back to 6.3 million years ago in Asia. While excavating fossils in a remote area of southwestern Tibet, Tseng's team uncovered a nearly complete skull of a previously unknown species of big cat, which they called *Panthera blytheae*. They determined that the skull—the oldest big cat fossil ever found—belonged to a direct ancestor of the snow leopard. This made snow leopards the most ancient of all the big cats on the planet.

The snow leopard's ancient origins have placed it at the center of Himalayan culture and protected it from

Family squabbles help cubs learn skills that build confidence and help them protect themselves as adults.

Snow leopards have many allies, as about 80 percent of the people living in the big cats' habitat practice Tibetan Buddhism.

people who encounter it as an occasional predator of domestic livestock. Yet the snow leopard remains an endangered species. Snow leopard fur is one of the most valuable furs in the world. One pelt (the skin with the fur still attached) may sell for as much as $60,000, and its body parts are used in some traditional Chinese medicines. Despite the cat's legal protection worldwide, most areas lack the resources to enforce laws.

For example, just 40 to 50 conservation officers, many working only part-time, patrol the rugged landscape of the Sanjiangyuan Nature Reserve along the eastern Tibetan Plateau. The area is roughly the size of the American state of Illinois and inhabited by about 76,000 farmers and herders. Poachers regularly outmaneuver the officers and are rarely caught. However, they may encounter other opposition: Buddhist teaching forbids the killing of sacred snow leopards, and Buddhist monks living amongst the cats actively protect them from poachers.

Hundreds of Buddhist monasteries are scattered throughout China, Tibet, and other snow leopard habitat. The monks who live in the monasteries not only patrol the mountains, but they also educate **indigenous** people

about the importance of environmental protection and encourage communities to report poaching. A study conducted by researchers from the Snow Leopard Trust determined that the monks' activities have had a significant influence on snow leopard conservation. Dr. Li Juan, a biologist from Peking University and leader of the study, believes that the monks' work, combined with cooperation from local and state authorities, could be the key to the snow leopard's future.

Another study of snow leopards is helping researchers learn how to help these big cats survive. Big-cat expert

Many Buddhist monasteries such as this one in Litang, China, are home to monks committed to protecting snow leopards.

Spring snowmelts prompt snow leopards to eat exposed vegetation, which is unusual for feline species.

Boone Smith went to the mountains of Afghanistan to capture snow leopards for a study led by New York's Wildlife Conservation Society. The first of its kind, the 2012 study was designed to use **satellite**-tracking collars to follow snow leopards' movements through their habitat. Highlights of Smith's trip to the Wakhan Corridor of Afghanistan— an area with an elevation of 11,000 feet (3,353 m)—were filmed for the National Geographic documentary *Snow Leopard of Afghanistan*.

Smith used a specialized trap to capture a snow leopard by the paw and immobilize it. Then a veterinarian shot the big cat with a tranquilizer dart to make it fall asleep. They immediately covered the cat's face so that bright light would not awaken it. A collar holding a **Global Positioning System** (GPS) tracking device was placed around the snow leopard's neck. Such GPS transmitters allow researchers to monitor animals in the wild using satellites to gather data on the animals' movements.

Understanding how snow leopards move through and use their habitat is helpful in devising ways of reducing conflicts between snow leopards and humans. Younger snow leopards are inexperienced hunters and are more likely to raid villages for domestic livestock than older cats. Villagers understand the risks associated with sharing snow leopard habitat. However, those risks are now increasing. Global climate change is causing glaciers to melt and thus prompting more vegetation to grow at higher altitudes. Herders allow their animals to graze in those places, pushing them and their predators into more confined areas higher up the mountains. Then, as snow leopards and wolves descend the mountains to escape the

Male yaks can carry roughly 220 pounds (99.8 kg) of supplies for Himalayan sheep and yak herders.

By 2080, a steadily warming climate could destroy up to 30 percent of current snow leopard habitat.

Felines produce milk that is richer in calcium than other mammals', helping their young develop strong bones and teeth.

winter snow, conflicts with humans increase.

Research on climate change's effects on snow leopard behavior is being conducted by a number of organizations. Dr. Rodney Jackson, who has been studying snow leopards for nearly four decades, founded the Snow Leopard Conservancy in 2000. This organization is particularly involved in research that helps humans live in harmony with snow leopards. While working with Mitchell Kelly on the "Silent Roar" episode, Jackson and his crew used infrared motion- and heat-sensing equipment to get never-before-seen footage of snow leopards hunting, scent-marking their home ranges, and mating. The footage also showed a mother snow leopard with two cubs.

In 2011, a team of scientists from the Panthera Corporation and the Snow Leopard Trust discovered two active snow leopard dens in Mongolia's Tost Mountains. While the mothers were away hunting, scientists weighed, measured, and photographed three cubs. Tiny microchips about the size of a grain of rice were injected under the cubs' skin for future identification. This type of research can help scientists learn more about den life and hunting habits.

Studying wild snow leopards is also invaluable for captive-breeding programs. About 70 North American zoos breed snow leopards. These big cats are vital to the health of their habitats. Species recovery programs, combined with local education and protection, can affect the future of snow leopards and their environments. We have only begun to unravel the secrets of the snow leopard, a fascinating big cat with more mysteries to reveal—if only it can survive the pressures of its changing world.

By the time cubs reach two years of age and are ready to leave their mother, they will look almost like her.

ANIMAL TALE: THE FIRST SNOW LEOPARD

In many cultures, stories are created to explain unusual occurrences or discoveries. In mid-1900s Siberia, a folk tale emerged about the connection between the origin of the snow leopard and an ancient mummy found buried in the mountains.

Long ago, a Scythian tribe lived in the foothills of the Altai Mountains. The tribal chief had one daughter, the Princess of Altai. She was the most beautiful girl in the land. One day, while she was picking herbs in the forest, she caught sight of a young man washing his horse's foot in a stream.

The princess approached the man, whose hair was white as snow and whose eyes were blue as the sky. He wore a heavy, white cloak over his shoulders. "What are you doing?" she asked him.

"My horse was injured by a thorn," the man told her.

"You are very kind to care for your horse in this manner," the princess said, for the Scythians were known to be impatient and even cruel to animals. She knew this man was different from her people.

From that day on, the princess and the man met by the stream nearly every day. The man showed the princess where to find the best herbs and how to appreciate the beauty of the animals. He took her to secret caves in the mountains. The princess had never before felt such happiness.

"Become my wife and live with me in the mountains," the man said to the princess.

"Yes, yes!" the princess replied, beaming with joy. The man took the princess to the top of the mountain where the Mountain Spirit joined the pair in marriage.

At daybreak, the princess awoke and could hardly wait to hurry back to her father to share the wonderful news.

Meanwhile, the Scythian chief felt the time had come for his daughter to marry, and he selected a noble warrior from a neighboring tribe. But the princess was nowhere to be found. "Where is my daughter?" he roared.

"Here," said the princess, arriving at her father's tent. She excitedly told her father that she had pledged herself to a man who lived on the mountain. This news enraged the chief. He sent his sons to find the man and kill him.

The princess cried out and begged her father to reconsider, but the order was given. The princess would be handed over to the neighboring tribe while her brothers raced toward the mountain.

Tearfully, the princess hurried to warn her husband. But when she reached the mountain, she discovered that she was too late. Her brothers had killed her husband. His beautiful white cloak lay on the ground covered with muddy hoof prints. The princess cried out in agony, calling to the Mountain Spirit to help her.

"I cannot restore his life," the Mountain Spirit said. "We will bury him so that his spirit will remain on the mountain forever." The Mountain Spirit put the man's cloak over the princess's shoulders. Instantly, the princess transformed into a spotted snow leopard.

Indeed, in 1969, the mummified body of a man was discovered in the frozen ground of a burial mound in the Altai Mountains. He lived more than 2,000 years ago. And to this day, the princess—the snow leopard—remains hidden on the highest snowy peaks.

GLOSSARY

captive-breeding – being bred and raised in a place from which escape is not possible

climate change – the gradual increase in Earth's temperature that causes changes in the planet's atmosphere, environments, and long-term weather conditions

cultures – particular groups in a society that share behaviors and characteristics that are accepted as normal by that group

domesticated – tamed to be kept as a pet or used as a work animal

evolved – gradually developed into a new form

extinct – having no living members

food chain – a system in nature in which living things are dependent on each other for food

fragmented – an organism's habitat having been broken up into scattered sections that may result in difficulty moving safely from one place to another

glands – organs in a human or animal body that produce chemical substances used by other parts of the body

Global Positioning System – a system of satellites, computers, and other electronic devices that work together to determine the location of objects or living things that carry a trackable device

indigenous – originating in a particular region or country

mammals – warm-blooded animals that have a backbone and hair or fur, give birth to live young, and produce milk to feed their young

migrate – to undertake a regular, seasonal journey from one place to another and then back again

mythology – a collection of myths, or popular, traditional beliefs or stories that explain how something came to be or that are associated with a person or object

nomadic – relating to a group of people or animals with no fixed home who move, often according to the seasons, in search of food, water, or grazing land

paleontologist – a person who studies fossils of animals, plants, and other organisms that existed long ago

poaching – hunting protected species of wild animals, even though doing so is against the law

retina – a layer or lining in the back of the eye that is sensitive to light

retractable – able to be drawn in from an extended position

satellite – a mechanical device launched into space; it may be designed to travel around Earth or toward other planets or the sun

---

SELECTED BIBLIOGRAPHY

Hunter, Don, ed. *Snow Leopard: Stories from the Roof of the World.* Boulder: University of Colorado Press, 2012.

Kelly, Mitchell, and Hugh Miles. "Silent Roar: Searching for the Snow Leopard." *Nature*, season 23, episode 5. Aired January 16, 2005. DVD. New York: Thirteen/WNET.

Macdonald, David W., and Andrew J. Loveridge, eds. *The Biology and Conservation of Wild Felids.* Oxford: Oxford University Press, 2010.

Montsion, Leah. "*Uncia uncia.*" Animal Diversity Web. http://animaldiversity.ummz.umich.edu/accounts/Uncia_uncia.

National Geographic. "Snow Leopard." http://animals.nationalgeographic.com/animals/mammals/snow-leopard/?source=A-to-Z.

Snow Leopard Trust. "Cat Facts." http://www.snowleopard.org/learn/cat-facts.

Sunquist, Fiona, and Mel Sunquist. *The Wild Cat Book.* Chicago: University of Chicago Press, 2014.

Note: Every effort has been made to ensure that any websites listed above were active at the time of publication. However, because of the nature of the Internet, it is impossible to guarantee that these sites will remain active indefinitely or that their contents will not be altered.

Few mountain-dwelling animals can match the speed and precision with which a snow leopard moves.

INDEX